Famous Lives

The Life of Cleopatra

By Kathleen Connors

Gareth Stevens
Publishing

Please visit our website, www.garethstevens.com. For a free color catalog of all our high-quality books, call toll free 1-800-542-2595 or fax 1-877-542-2596.

Library of Congress Cataloging-in-Publication Data

Connors, Kathleen.
Cleopatra / by Kathleen Connors.
 p. cm. — (Famous lives)
Includes index.
ISBN 978-1-4824-0387-9 (pbk.)
ISBN 978-1-4824-0388-6 (6-pack)
ISBN 978-1-4824-0384-8 (library binding)
1. Cleopatra, — Queen of Egypt, — -30 B.C. — Juvenile literature. 2. Egypt — History — 332-30 B.C. — Juvenile literature. 3. Queens — Egypt — Biography — Juvenile literature. I. Connors, Kathleen. II. Title.
DT92.7 C66 2014
932.021—dc23

First Edition

Published in 2014 by
Gareth Stevens Publishing
111 East 14th Street, Suite 349
New York, NY 10003

Copyright © 2014 Gareth Stevens Publishing

Designer: Nicholas Domiano
Editor: Kristen Rajczak

Photo credits: Cover, p. 1 A. Dagli Orti/De Agostini Picture Library/Getty Images; p. 5 DEA PICTURE LIBRARY/De Agostini Picture Library/Getty Images; p. 7 A. Benini/The Bridgeman Art Library/ Getty Images; p. 9 Hulton Archive/Getty Images; p. 11 GERARD JULIEN/AFP/Getty Images; p. 13 Max Alexander/Dorling Kindersley/Getty Images; p. 15 Peter Willi/Superstock/Getty Images; p. 17 Mansell/Time & Life Pictures/Getty Images; p. 19 Pompeo Girolamo Batoni/The Bridgeman Art Library/Getty Images; p. 21 Um Sixtyfour/Shutterstock.com.

Printed in the United States of America

CPSIA compliance information: Batch #CW14GS: For further information contact Gareth Stevens, New York, New York at 1-800-542-2595.

Contents

Boldface words appear in the glossary.

The Last Pharaoh

Cleopatra was an Egyptian queen. Her rule was the last before Egypt became part of Rome. While queen, she fought to keep control of Egypt's many lands.

Cleopatra was born in 69 BC. Her father was Ptolemy (TAHL-uh-mee) XII, an Egyptian **pharaoh**. However, her family wasn't Egyptian! They were from a part of Greece called Macedonia.

7

Ready to Rule

Cleopatra's father died in 51 BC. Cleopatra was the oldest child, but a woman couldn't rule alone. She had to rule along with her younger brother, Ptolemy XIII.

Ptolemy XIII

9

Cleopatra and her brother struggled with each other for power. She asked the Roman leader Julius Caesar for help. He fell in love with Cleopatra and helped her retake the **throne**.

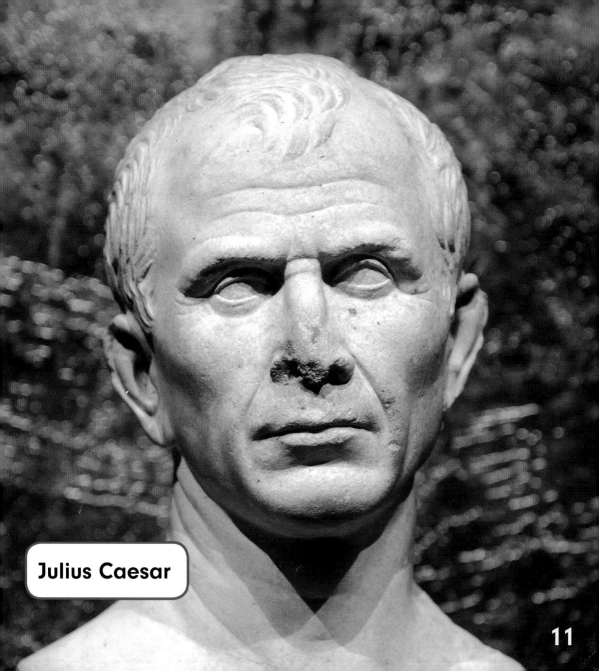

Julius Caesar

Cleopatra's brother died, and she had to rule along with her other younger brother. But Cleopatra and Caesar were still in love and had a son named Caesarion in 47 BC. He became king in 44 BC when Cleopatra's brother died.

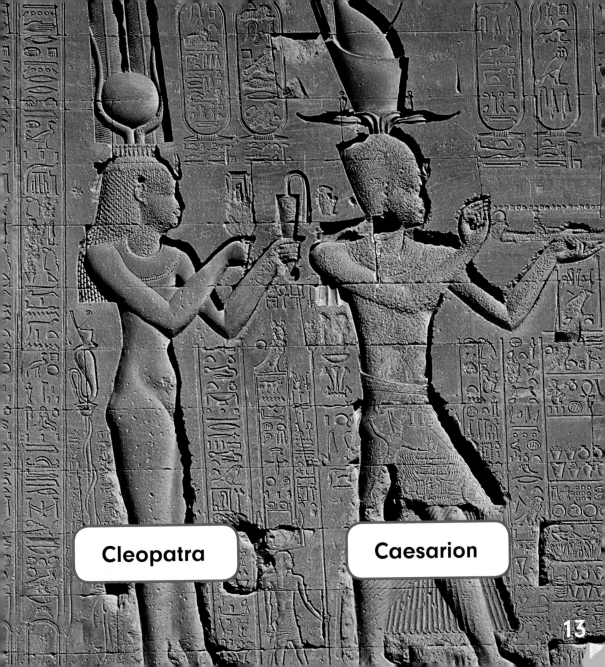

Cleopatra

Caesarion

Roman Danger

Julius Caesar was killed in 44 BC. Two men fought to **succeed** him, Marc Antony and Octavian, Caesar's **adopted** son. Antony met Cleopatra in 42 BC. She wanted him to help keep Egypt **independent** from Rome.

Marc Antony

Cleopatra

Love and War

Antony and Cleopatra worked together for many years. They also had three children. In 34 BC, Antony angered Octavian, who was still his **rival**. Antony said Caesarion should be Rome's ruler instead of Octavian.

17

Antony gave his children Roman land, too. Octavian blamed Cleopatra. He **conquered** Egypt in 31 BC. Antony thought Cleopatra had been killed. He died, just as news came that she was still alive.

Egypt's End

Cleopatra died in 30 BC. She likely didn't want to be taken by Octavian. It's not certain how she died. Many stories say she died after letting a snake bite her.

Timeline

- **69 BC**—Cleopatra is born.
- **51 BC**—Cleopatra and her brother begin to rule.
- **47 BC**—Caesarion is born.
- **44 BC**—Caesar is killed. Caesarion becomes king.
- **42 BC**—Cleopatra meets Marc Antony.
- **31 BC**—Octavian conquers Egypt.
- **30 BC**—Cleopatra dies.

Glossary

adopted: to have been made part of a family

conquer: to take over

independent: free

pharaoh: an Egyptian ruler

rival: one of two or more people trying to get what only one can have

succeed: to come after another

throne: royal power

For More Information

Books

Costain, Meredith. *Ancient Egypt.* New York, NY: PowerKids Press, 2013.

Twist, Clint. *Cleopatra: Queen of Egypt.* Somerville, MA: Candlewick Press, 2012.

Websites

Ancient Egypt for Kids

egypt.mrdonn.org/
Use this site to find out more about the ancient Egyptians.

The Search for Cleopatra

ngm.nationalgeographic.com/2011/07/cleopatra/ garrett-photography
See National Geographic's photographs of artifacts showing Cleopatra and her time in ancient Egypt.

Index

Famous Lives

Levels: GR: I;
DRA: 16; EI: 15

ISBN: 978-1-4824-0387-9
6-pack ISBN: 978-1-4824-0388-6

CYF

GS
Gareth
Stevens